EXPLORING EARTH'S · BIOMES ·

TEMPERATE DECIDUOUS
FOREST

APRIL PULLEY SAYRE

TWENTY-FIRST CENTURY BOOKS

A Division of Henry Holt and Company
• New York •

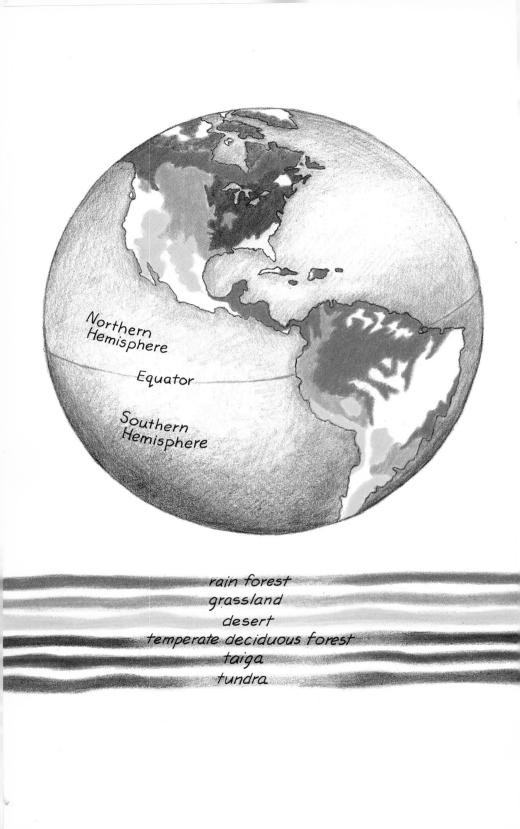

Northern
Hemisphere

Equator

Southern
Hemisphere

rain forest
grassland
desert
temperate deciduous forest
taiga
tundra

INTRODUCTION

Take a look at the earth as a whole and you'll see its surface can be divided into living communities called biomes. Desert, rain forest, tundra, taiga, temperate deciduous forest, grassland, and polar desert are some of the main terrestrial biomes—biomes on land. Each biome has particular kinds of plants and animals living in it. Scientists also identify other biomes not mentioned here, including aquatic biomes—biomes of lakes, streams, and the sea.

When their boundaries are drawn on a globe, terrestrial biomes look like horizontal bands stacked up from Pole to Pole. Starting from the equator and moving outward toward the Poles, you'll find rain forests, grasslands, deserts, and grasslands once again. Then things change a little. The next biomes we think of—temperate deciduous forests, taiga, and tundra—exist only in the Northern Hemisphere. Why is this true? Well, if you look in the Southern Hemisphere, you'll see there's very little land in the regions where these biomes would supposedly lie. There's simply nowhere for these biomes to exist! Conditions on small pieces of land—islands and peninsulas—that lie in these areas are greatly affected by sea conditions and are very different from those on continents.

But why do biomes generally develop in these bands? The answer lies in the earth's climate and geology. Climate is affected by the angle at which sunlight hits the earth. At the equator, sunlight passes through the atmosphere and hits the earth straight on, giving it its full energy. At the Poles, sunlight must pass through more atmosphere and it hits the earth at an angle, with less energy per square foot. Other factors also influence where biomes lie: the bands of rising and falling air that circulate around the planet; the complex weather systems created by jutting mountains, deep valleys, and cold currents; the glaciers that have scoured the lands in years past; and the activities of humans. This makes biome boundaries less regular than the simplified bands described above.

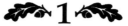

THE TEMPERATE DECIDUOUS FOREST BIOME

No matter how many times you've seen them, the bright colors of fall leaves in a temperate deciduous forest come as something of a shock. Each year it seems the bare branches of winter, and the greens of spring and summer, make you forget just how colorful leaves can be.

Then, in a few crisp, cool days, the forest turns color. Tree and shrub species emerge, now distinct in their fall finery. Red sugar maples, purple sweet gums, deep red oaks, rainbow-colored sumacs, and other trees create a patchwork of color. Red-toned Virginia creeper and poison ivy sew it all together, spiraling up tree trunks, and creeping along the ground.

Leaf color is among the most remarkable features of the temperate deciduous forest, especially in North America. But what gives this forest its name is what leaves do after their colorful show: they fall.

Millions of tons of leaves, once held aloft by branches, are suddenly set free, to swirl in the wind, to float in streams, to settle on the ground. This sudden movement of vegetation, from branches to the ground, is one of the most remarkable, gigantic energy transfers on the planet. Yet it happens in any temperate deciduous forest, from England's legendary Sherwood Forest to New York City's Central Park.

Shedding leaves all at once is called deciduousness. It only occurs in deciduous trees. In contrast, evergreen trees, such as the conifers of the taiga, keep their leaves some-

*North America's temperate deciduous forest
displays fabulous leaf color each autumn.*

times for five or more years. Some evergreen trees grow
scattered within the temperate deciduous forest. But most
of the trees are deciduous, giving the forest its name.

Stretching over the eastern half of the United States,
parts of eastern Asia, and western Europe, temperate deciduous forests cover a vast territory. Like desert or tundra, the
temperate deciduous forest is a biome—a geographic area
that has a certain kind of climate and a certain community
of plants and animals. The temperate deciduous forest
biome is known for its deciduousness, its many tree species,
its abundance of wildlife, and its rich, fertile soil.

There's also another kind of deciduous forest *not*
covered in this book. Tropical deciduous forests, such as
those in Central America, also have broad-leafed trees
that lose their leaves on a regular basis. But these trees
generally lose their leaves during dry seasons. Tropical
deciduous forests have warmer temperatures and a different soil and climate from temperate deciduous forests. And,
of course, these forests occur only in the tropics, not in the
temperate zone. In this book we will use the word *deciduous*
to refer only to temperate deciduous forests.

TYPES

Temperate deciduous forests are classified according to the dominant tree species. These forest types are called associations. There are many different associations. Some of the most common are:

- Oak / Hickory.
- Beech / Maple.
- Mixed mesophytic. (This forest association is mixed, meaning it can be dominated by any one of ten or so species. It is mesophytic, meaning it grows in an environment with a moderate amount of available water.)

TEMPERATURES

- Air temperature changes markedly at night and during the year.
- Average yearly temperature is at least 75°F (24°C) but can be as high as 86°F (30°C), depending on the forest's altitude. (At higher altitudes, temperatures are cooler.)

WEATHER

- Relative humidity is high: 60 to 80 percent.
- The temperate deciduous forest experiences four noticeable seasons of about equal length: spring, summer, winter, and fall.
- There is no dry season; precipitation falls throughout the year.
- Deciduous forests average 30 to 80 inches (80 to 200 centimeters) of precipitation per year.

SOIL

- Deciduous forest soils vary, but are generally rich in nutrients. The topsoil layer is deep with a thick humus layer—

Temperate Deciduous Forest
Throughout the World

North America
Europe
Asia
Africa
South America
Australia
Antarctica

a layer of well-decomposed plant and animal matter—
and a fairly thick layer of decaying leaves on top.

- Temperate deciduous forest nutrients are stored mostly in the decaying leaves and in the soil. Soil is often good for farming.

PLANTS

- Plant biomass—the total weight of plant matter—for a given area is comparatively high: higher than grassland, desert, or tundra.
- Plants are arranged in a layered forest structure with a canopy, an understory, a shrub layer, and an herb layer.
- Many species of trees, vines, and herbs grow within these forests.
- Trees grow to 3 to 5 feet (1 to 1.5 meters) in diameter, 80 to 100 feet (25 to 30 meters) in height.

ANIMALS

- Wildlife is abundant; moderate species diversity.
- Fewer large mammals than in the taiga but smaller mammals such as raccoons, skunks, foxes, voles, and mice are more common.
- Amphibians such as salamanders are particularly numerous.

2
TEMPERATE DECIDUOUS FOREST IN NORTH AMERICA

Stretching across the eastern United States, the deciduous forest is widespread and varied. Most of it has been logged, burned, or cleared for farming at one time or another in the last two centuries. So very little exists in its original state, with wide-trunked, towering trees. But even secondary forests—the forests that have regrown in these areas—can be varied, diverse, and beautiful, supporting wildlife that includes bears, deer, squirrels, and birds.

If you visit a temperate deciduous forest in the Ozarks, you'll find it looks quite different from the one in New England. That's because each region's forest is dominated by different trees. In the Ozarks, oak and hickory dominate the scene, while in the north–central forest region, sugar maple and American beech are the most plentiful. And in the rich forests of the Appalachian Mountains, any one of ten or so tree species can be dominant.

Many factors limit the spread of the temperate deciduous forest. In the north, cold weather favors the growth of taiga conifers rather than temperate deciduous forest trees. To the west, where the plains begin, it's too dry for forest, and prairie grows instead. And in the southeast and the south, sandy soils and frequent fires create conditions where pines grow better than deciduous trees. Even within the biome's geographic range, the slope of the land and the path of water and fire can create a patchwork of fields, wetlands, streams, ponds, and other features within the forest.

- At the northern reaches of the forest, in New England, the upper Midwest, and portions of southern Canada, taiga mingles with the temperate deciduous forest. This transitional forest is a 150-mile- (250-kilometer-) wide ecotone where broad-leafed, deciduous trees, such as sugar maple, birch, beech, and hemlock, mix with conifers such as spruce, pine, and fir.
- From Minnesota and Michigan on into New England is the pine forest of Paul Bunyan fame. This area, sometimes ılled the northern pine forest, was created by a drought in the 1500s that favored the growth of pine trees rather than deciduous trees. Now that climatic conditions have changed, and there is less land clearing and burning—which favors pines—the forest is regrowing with oak, maple, beech, and other deciduous trees.
- In the northeastern, southeastern, and southern United States lie many forests dominated by pine trees. These are called disturbance forests. When not disturbed by lumbering, land clearing, drought, or fires, much of this land supports oak and other temperate deciduous trees. But this land is disturbed, again and again. So it remains covered in pine trees.

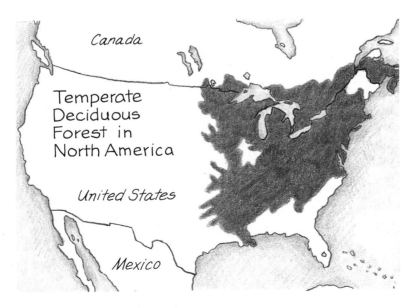

Canada

Temperate
Deciduous
Forest in
North America

United States

Mexico

3

TEMPERATE DECIDUOUS FOREST WEATHER, CLIMATE, AND GEOLOGY

It's raining in the forest, and, all of a sudden, *zap!* Lightning hits a tree. Electricity runs down the wet sap underneath the tree's bark, heating the sap until it boils, and *phloom!* Steam explodes out the side of the tree, ripping a long strip of bark off the trunk. The heat ignites a spark that begins a fire.

Weather events can have dramatic, drastic effects on the forest, like when lightning starts a fire, wind blows down a tree, or hard rain helps fall leaves drop. But just as important, if less dramatic, is the effect overall weather and climate have throughout the year, and year to year. These forces shape the life of the forest. That's why knowing about the weather, climate, and soils of the temperate deciduous forest helps scientists understand the "big picture"—why forest animals and plants live the way they do.

ZONES AND BOUNDARIES

As indicated by their name, temperate deciduous forests lie in the temperate zone. In the Northern Hemisphere this zone stretches from the Tropic of Cancer to the Arctic Circle. Roughly, that's from just below Florida all the way to northern Canada. (In the Southern Hemisphere, the temperate zone stretches from the Tropic of Capricorn to the Antarctic Circle, but very little deciduous forest exists there because there is very little land in those latitudes.)

Temperate deciduous forests don't fill up the whole temperate zone. Deserts, prairies, and taiga are found there, too. So what controls where temperate deciduous forest grows and where it does not? Many factors. In the north, cold temperatures favor the growth of taiga conifers over deciduous, broad-leafed trees. In the west, rainfall decreases, so prairie plants, which can handle the dryness, take over. In the south and southeast, and in the northeast and historically the Midwest, sandy soils and frequent fires favor the growth of pines instead of broad-leafed deciduous trees. In the middle, where none of these conditions is extreme, temperate deciduous forest grows.

WEATHER

Chances are, if you're a weathercaster in a temperate region such as the eastern United States, your forecasts will often miss the mark. Unlike the tropics, where temperatures change little day to day, the temperate region's weather can be a storm of contrasts. Each month you can expect typical average temperatures and certain types of weather. In January, temperatures average between 10°F (-12°C) and 30°F (-1.1°C). In July, temperatures average between 36°F (2.2°C) and 81°F (27°C). But temperature and humidity can change in a day, in an hour, in a few minutes. What will happen in a given day can be hard to predict.

The Humidity Blanket   From day to night, temperatures in the temperate deciduous forest do not drop as much as they do in the desert. That's because the forest's 60 to 80 percent relative humidity helps to moderate temperature change. A moist blanket of air insulates the forest, helping keep heat in the forest at night. In daytime this insulation prevents the forest from warming up too quickly. In contrast, deserts—which have little humidity—warm up quickly during the day and cool off very rapidly at night.

Plenty of Precip   Temperate deciduous forests do not experience a rainy season and dry season as do tropical rain

Camping in the forest is a favorite pastime for many people.

forests. Instead, precipitation—whether rainfall or snow—is distributed fairly evenly throughout the year. Overall, temperate deciduous forest receives more precipitation than any other major biome except rain forest. Yearly snowfall ranges from 8 to 96 inches (20 to 244 centimeters). While average yearly precipitation—rain and melted-down snow combined—is 32 to 80 inches (81 to 203 centimeters).

The Four Seasons   The seasons of a deciduous forest—spring, summer, fall, and winter—are all about the same length. Winter, the coldest season, has short days that have only a few hours of sunlight to warm the forest. At that time of year, cold Arctic air reaches far down into the United States, bringing snowstorms to the northern parts of deciduous forest. In spring, as days lengthen, there's an overall warming. Cold air from the Arctic and warm air from the Gulf of Mexico clash, often creating stormy, changeable weather. Then, in summer, temperatures and day length peak, and warm air masses may settle over the forest, creating hot, muggy conditions. Fall brings lower temperatures, as the hours of daylight decrease and temperatures begin to plummet. Winter returns and the cycle continues.

WHAT MAKES THE SEASONS?

What makes summer days long and warm, and winter days cold and short? Why are there seasons at all? The answer to both questions involves the positions of the sun and the earth. Planet earth is tilted on its axis relative to the sun. As a result, during certain parts of the earth's orbit, the North Pole and Northern Hemisphere are closer to the sun. During other parts of the earth's orbit, the South Pole and Southern Hemisphere are closer to the sun. When the Northern Hemisphere is at its closest to the sun, it is summer there. Meanwhile, it's winter in the Southern Hemisphere. At the opposite part of the earth's orbit, when the Northern Hemisphere is at its farthest from the sun, the seasons are reversed. Fall and spring occur in the "in-between" times when the earth is between one extreme or the other.

But what actually causes the changes we associate with the seasons? The sun's energy. When the sun is closer to a

Winter in Northern Hemisphere

The forecast for the Southern Hemisphere calls for a heat wave, with temperatures around 80°F. ..

Summer in Northern Hemisphere

There is a chance of snow in the Southern Hemisphere, with temperatures around 25°F. ..

certain part of the earth, it is summer there. The sun's energy travels a shorter distance through the atmosphere and more of it falls on each square foot of ground. Because of the tilt of the earth, there are also more hours of daylight each day, so that part of the planet receives more energy overall. Therefore, sunlight affects the temperatures we experience each season. Portions of the energy that arrive also affect plants' abilities to carry out photosynthesis.

SOILS

Temperate deciduous forest soils vary. But in general, they are fertile, with plenty of minerals and organic matter. Much of it is brown, though it may also be gray or red. Warm temperatures prevent the ground from permanently freezing, as it does in the tundra. So plant roots can reach deeply, gaining the minerals and water they need from the soil. Because plants can grow so well in these soils, much of the temperate deciduous forest has been cleared to grow crops.

Deep Dirt Compared to tropical rain forest, temperate deciduous forest has soil that is relatively deep and fertile. On the temperate deciduous forest floor, most leaves decompose fairly rapidly, within a year. (An exception is oak leaves, which may pile up several inches thick and take two to three years to break down.) Underneath these leaves lies humus, a deep layer of decomposed leaves and other organic matter that has been thoroughly mixed and broken down by earthworms, insects, fungi, and bacteria. Under this layer, tiny pieces of rock mix with organic matter to form soil. In this biome, soil nutrients and minerals are constantly being mixed by seeping water, seasonal freezing and thawing, the movement of plant roots, and burrowing animals. As a result, minerals and organic matter from the humus above, and minerals dissolved by groundwater from rock below, all help replenish the soil.

A WRINKLED LAND

Featuring cliffs, crags, mountains, valleys, rolling hills, and plateaus, the land beneath the temperate deciduous forest is a wrinkled place. The bumpy backbone of the region is the Appalachian Mountains, running south from New York to Alabama. The peaks of this ancient, worn-down mountain range are much lower than those of the Rockies, but are still impressive. On each side of the Appalachian Mountains, gently rolling foothills spread out and then flatten, east toward the Atlantic coast, and west toward the Mississippi River. Streams, rivers, and springs erode and pattern the land, bringing water to these forests.

ANCIENT HISTORY

The temperate deciduous forest has not always existed exactly where it does today. For thousands of years, New England and portions of the northern Midwest as far south as central Ohio and Indiana were covered by ice. After the

Hiking on the Appalachian Trail is a great way
to explore the temperate deciduous forest.

glacial ice melted, about 10,000 years ago, plants, and eventually forests, began growing on these lands once again. The first forests were taiga, made up of conifers such as spruce and fir. In many places, these spruce and fir forests were replaced by pine. Later on, as the climate warmed, deciduous forests replaced or intermixed with these spruce/fir and pine forests.

Because of their ice-covered history, the forests of New England and the Great Lakes region are comparatively young. Deciduous trees there are mostly oaks, beeches, maples, and aspens, which are among the first deciduous trees to colonize newly revealed northern land. The ancient, less disturbed forests of the southern Appalachian region have many more tree species—even dozens—in some rich, diverse pockets of forest.

4
TEMPERATE DECIDUOUS FOREST PLANTS

Temperate deciduous forests experience some of the best growing conditions on earth. Good soil, lots of nutrients, plentiful rain, and a long growing season make these forests lush and varied. Trees grow to heights of 80 to 100 feet (25 to 30 meters). Virginia creeper, bittersweet, poison ivy, and other vines run along the ground and twine up trees, stretching for hundreds of yards. Wildflowers bloom in profusion. And mushrooms, mosses, and lichens fill in the spaces, creating spots of color and unusual shapes on rocks, trees, and the forest floor.

'TIS THE SEASON

Plants in these forests adjust their growth and activity to the seasons of the year. In spring, in maple woodlands, trout lilies, spring beauties, and other low-growing wildflowers emerge. These flowers, called spring ephemerals, take advantage of the strong sunlight available before the trees leaf out. Then, once the tree leaves are out and shading the forest floor, many of these plants' leaves wither and die, leaving the plants' roots or bulbs alive underground, ready to grow the next year.

In summer, trees are green and leafy, so large-leafed plants adapted to low light conditions prevail on the shady forest floor. Shrubs and short trees flower, forming berries in late summer and early fall. Then, as days grow short and temperatures gradually decrease, tree leaves turn color and drop. For nearly six months, most temperate deciduous forest plants are leafless, and seemingly lifeless. But in spring, the cycle begins again.

TRICKS OF SEASONED COMPETITORS

In the forest, plants compete with one another for light, space, and nutrients. And they adjust to the seasons as well. A few of the remarkable ways they adapt to these demands are described below.

Presto, Plants!   Spring wildflowers can appear as if by magic, complete with leaves and flowers, in only a few days. How do they do it? By forming their leaves ahead of time, underground. When the time is right, they push a rosette of tightly packed leaves up through the soil. Then they open up and presto! Plants. (Dandelions form the same way, which explains why they appear so quickly on lawns.) Other plants use additional tactics to get a head start on spring. Some trees form tiny leaves the previous fall, then keep them wrapped tightly in buds during the winter. And a plant called skunk cabbage actually generates heat, melting snow and frozen ground so it can emerge earlier than other plants in wet, swampy forest.

Made in the Shade   Small plants close to the ground generally have broad, thin, nonoverlapping leaves. These leaves are good at gathering light in shady conditions. This helps plants survive on the shady forest floor. Even trees may grow broad, thin, "shade leaves" on the inner parts of the tree where outer leaves block most of the sunlight.

Toughen Up   If you expose a plant to low temperatures in summer, it's more likely to die than if you expose it to the same temperatures in winter. That's because in the fall

Skunk cabbage is one of the first plants
to emerge in the springtime forest.

plants "toughen up." They undergo a process called hardening that prepares their tissues for the rigors of winter.

THE WHY, WHEN, AND HOW OF LEAF FALL

In an acre (two-fifths of a hectare) of forest, an estimated ten million leaves fall in autumn. But why, when, and how does this happen?

The Why   The why of leaf fall at first seems simple. Most broad leaves fall because winter conditions are too harsh for them to survive. But what exactly is it about winter that makes broad leaves impractical to maintain? Is it the snow that could build up on a tree and break its branches? Or is it the cold temperatures that could freeze a plant's fluids? The answer may surprise you.

Although both the snow buildup and cold are important, scientists believe drought—lack of water—may be even more of a problem for plants in winter. At low temper-

Thousands head to temperate deciduous forest regions to enjoy the fall foliage each year.

atures, plants have a hard time absorbing the water they need to maintain broad leaves, which tend to lose a lot of water. Trees also have a hard time carrying out photosynthesis in cold temperatures. (Evergreen trees, which keep their leaves in winter, tend to have narrow needle-shaped leaves that lose very little water.)

The When   What exactly triggers leaves to fall? Scientists believe almost 20 different factors determine when leaves will fall. Temperature, day length, and moisture are some of the more important factors. The exact timing of leaf color turn and leaf fall can vary from year to year and species to species.

The How   How leaves turn color and fall is an easier question to answer. During fall, trees grow a layer of cells, called the abscission layer, between the twig and the leaf stem. This layer cuts off the leaf's supplies of water and nutrients so the leaf begins to shut down production. Chlorophyll, which is green, is used up and disappears from the leaf. This reveals yellow and orange pigments that have been present in the leaf all year long, but were hidden by the chlorophyll. Later, some of the sugars in the leaves of trees such as oaks and maples are made into reddish pigments that add to the colorful fall show. Once completely shut down, leaves fall, breaking off at the abscission layer.

PLANT PIGMENT EXPERIMENT

Amazingly enough, the yellow and orange pigments that show up in fall leaves are there all year long. This experi-ment shows how you can demonstrate that is true. It uses a technique called chromatography, which separates the heavier pigments from the lighter ones. It separates the green pigments found in a leaf from the other pigments revealed in fall.

Materials:
- Rubbing alcohol or acetone (nail polish remover) *Handle these chemicals carefully. Read warning labels and follow the directions on the bottles. These chemicals can be hazardous.*
- Small glass jar
- Several green leaves from different trees
- Pencil
- Ruler
- Paper clip
- Filter paper (a paper coffee filter will do)

1. Cut a strip of filter paper $1\frac{1}{2}$ inches (4 centimeters) wide and 4 inches (10 centimeters) long.

2. Lay a leaf on top of the filter paper and rub the leaf with the pencil so that you make a green spot on the center of the filter paper $\frac{3}{4}$ inch (2 centimeters) from the bottom of the strip. This will be your leaf pigment sample.

3. Using the paper clip, hang the filter paper from a pencil laid across the lip of the jar. Note where the bottom of the filter paper hangs in the jar.

4. Take the filter paper back out of the jar and pour enough

rubbing alcohol or acetone into the jar so it will just touch the bottom of the filter paper when you replace it. Now hang the filter paper back in the jar.

5. Check to make sure the alcohol or acetone is touching the bottom of the filter paper, but not the green dot of plant sample.

6. Let the experiment sit for one-half hour or so. The green pigment in the sample should have traveled upward with the alcohol or acetone moving up the paper. You should be able to see where it stopped. A yellowish streak continuing beyond where the green stopped indicates the presence of another pigment in the leaf. Each band of color on the paper indicates a pigment.

7. Repeat the experiment with other leaves.

Did all your samples have pigments "hidden" in the leaves? How many bands of pigment were present in each plant? Were they the same bands, the same distance from the sample, or were they in different positions?

For further experimentation, you can use plant parts, such as carrots, beets, flower petals, or cabbage. To make your plant samples of these, the pencil rubbing technique may not work. Instead, you can boil a piece of the plant in a small amount of water for 15 minutes. Use a drop of the water for your plant sample on the filter paper. Let the drop dry before beginning the chromatography.

POLLINATION

What plants can't do for themselves, they enlist the wind and animals to do for them. In the case of pollination, plants need to exchange genetic material contained in pollen so they can produce seeds with many different genetic traits. The yellow powder you might have seen on sidewalks and cars in spring is pollen, carried by wind from one tree to another. Using wind to carry pollen is very hit-or-miss. That's why many plants let animals be their couriers. By

Pollen baskets on a honeybee's legs help it to gather pollen for making honey.

producing sweet nectar, the plants attract insects or birds to their flowers. When the bird or insect sticks its tongue or proboscis into a flower for a sip, pollen is dabbed on its body. This pollen may rub off or fall off into the other flowers the animal visits. In that way the flowers obtain one another's pollen to produce seed.

Flowers advertise to attract pollinators. Colorful flowers help attract hummingbirds, butterflies, and moths. Stripes, contrasting colors, dots, and other flower patterns guide insects to the flower's pollen and nectar spots. Some of these markings reflect ultraviolet light, which is invisible to humans, but visible to bees. And to attract flies, the flowers of skunk cabbage, red trillium, and jack-in-the-pulpit give off a stinky odor, reminiscent of rotting meat. This scent attracts flies, which normally lay their eggs on dead and decaying animals so their young can hatch and eat the meat. When the flies lay eggs on the stinky flowers, they do the flower a service. As they are laying their eggs on these flowers, they accidentally pick up and deposit pollen. (The fly larvae, however, will be out of luck, because there will be no rotten meat to eat!)

THE BATTLE OF THE PLANTS

If you've ever been stung by nettles, snagged by thorns, or irritated by poison ivy, you've experienced plant defenses firsthand. Plants may seem passive, but their defenses can be quite effective, even against big, bumbling creatures such as humans. Thick bark, sharp thorns, stinging hairs, and irritating chemicals all discourage hungry plant eaters. And some plants can wage chemical warfare against one another. Black walnut trees have a potent toxin in their shells, leaves, and roots. This toxin kills the roots of trees trying to grow into the soil near the black walnut. A tomato plant growing 80 feet (24 meters) away may be affected, and the toxin can stay in the soil for years, even after the tree is removed.

THE WONDER OF TREES

A tree is a remarkable bit of plumbing. Inside it, long strings of cells, stacked end to end, create piping called xylem that carries water hundreds of feet into the air, to the leaves. Another type of piping, called phloem, carries sap, the sugary food made in the leaves, to other parts of the plant.

Wider and Wider As a tree grows, it grows not only upward, but outward, forming new cells in rings around its center. The outer parts of the wood are the ones that are alive. In an old tree, the dark heartwood in the center, clogged with the tree's waste products, no longer carries sap. Even if its insides rot, a tree can live by the activity of its outer bark and wood. But the heartwood provides support for the weight of the tree and so once it rots, a tree is much more likely to fall.

Ring upon Ring If you cut a cross section into a tree trunk in the temperate deciduous forest, you can discover the tree's age by its rings. How is this possible? In the spring, a

Tree rings provide a permanent record scientists can examine for clues about climate conditions stretching back hundreds of years.

tree grows quickly, creating wide, light-colored cells that show up as light springwood. Later in the season, stronger, denser summerwood is formed. One band of dark and one band of light together signifies one year of growth. The width of a ring indicates how good a growing season it was. Scientists have studied the rings in trees to find out about droughts, rainy seasons, fires, and weather and climatic conditions reaching back hundreds and thousands of years.

TREE DISEASE TRAGEDY

A hundred years ago, an estimated one out of every four hardwood trees in Appalachia was an American chestnut. Dark-trunked, massive, and reaching to 80 feet (24 meters), chestnuts were well-loved trees, providing shade and valu-

Like the chestnut blight, gypsy moths were accidentally brought to America from overseas. Forest managers wage a constant battle to protect oaks, elms, and pines from these insect pests.

able wood. The nuts were a major food source for people and wild animals. And tannin, a chemical used in the tanning of leather, was extracted from chestnut bark in large quantities.

Today, American chestnuts survive only as isolated stumps, with a few small sprouts. In the early 1900s, a fungus called chestnut blight arrived in America, presumably from cargo brought into a port in New York City. Traveling on wind, carried by rain, and stuck on birds' feet as they flew from tree to tree, the fungal spores spread quickly. Within 20 years the fungus had spread far and wide, leaving dead and dying chestnut trees on hillsides all over the eastern United States. In less than 40 years, blight virtually wiped out the population of American chestnut trees. Various species of oak trees filled in the forest gaps where the chestnut trees had been.

Other tree diseases and insect plagues challenge foresters as well. Dogwoods—an important berry tree in temperate deciduous forests—are being attacked by a disease and are declining. Gypsy moths, whose caterpillars eat the leaves of oaks and other trees, have repeatedly defoliated large areas of forest from New England southward. And Dutch elm disease has wiped out millions of elm trees in the United States and Canada. Today, scientists are still working to develop strains of trees that are resistant to these diseases.

WHY ARE FORESTS SO MESSY?

With old logs still standing, fallen logs rotting, and leaves lying around, the deciduous forest might look rather messy to some people. But unlike your room at home, this is one mess that should not be cleaned up. That's because none of this dead and decaying matter goes to waste. Standing dead trees, called snags, are "home sweet home" for owls, woodpeckers, raccoons, beetles, and other creatures that live inside them. Fallen, rotting logs are havens for insects, and shelter for salamanders, lizards, and toads. Leaf litter and branches, logs, and dead animals on the forest floor are eventually turned into soil by earthworms, beetles, fungi, and microorganisms. These decomposers not only break down dead plant and animal matter, but serve as food for other creatures large and small.

Much of the nutrient wealth of temperate deciduous forests is in the leaf litter on the forest floor, and the humus below. (This is different from tropical forests, where the nutrient wealth of the forest is held in the living trees.) If the forest floor is not continually replenished by leaves, branches, and other dead matter, the soil will become less fertile. That's why removing the undergrowth, the rotting material, and the leaves from the forest floor is generally not a good idea.

5
TEMPERATE DECIDUOUS FOREST ANIMALS

On a summer evening in the temperate deciduous forest, the best way to find animals is to listen. What sounds like people whistling, babies burping, and kids rubbing their hands across balloons is likely to be a frog chorus in full swing. What seems to be a very loud sneeze may be a deer's snorting call. And that pulsing *"katy-DID, katy-DIDn't"* is likely to be insects called katydids, rubbing their wings together to start their night of song.

Just judging by the din, you can tell these forests are rich with wildlife. From acrobatic squirrels, to fast-flying birds, to slow-moving opossums, wildlife in temperate deciduous forest is plentiful and varied in form and behavior. In this biome, animals have adapted to the four seasons. Winters may not be as cold as they are on the frigid, windswept tundra. And summer days may not be as hot and dry as in a sandy, sizzling desert. But life in the temperate deciduous forest is still a challenge, because animals must adapt to a yearlong, ever-shifting set of living conditions.

DEALING WITH WINTER
Despite their relatively mild climate, temperate deciduous forests get their share of cold winter weather. For four to seven months, the trees are leafless, and food is relatively scarce. To adapt to these conditions, animals either migrate, hibernate, or find some other way to endure the winter.

Migrators   Almost 70 percent of spring birds in the temperate deciduous forest are Neotropical migrants, meaning they spend most of the year in the tropics in South or Central America. In spring, these birds fly hundreds or thousands of miles north to the temperate deciduous forest. There they spend the summer raising young and taking advantage of the forest's summertime insect, seed, nectar, and berry feast. But as the weather turns cold, they fly south for the winter.

Hibernators   Other animals, such as bats, mice, and woodchucks, stay for the winter and hibernate. When in hibernation, an animal's body functions actually slow down, increasing its endurance of cold, and eliminating its need to find food and water. Deep in burrows, or back in caves, these creatures can "chill out" undisturbed. And that's important. Because if creatures such as bats and turtles are awakened during their winter hibernation, they can die. They use so much energy waking up that they often don't have enough energy to survive the rest of the winter.

Some animals, such as chipmunks and badgers, enter a sleepy state called torpor that is close to, but not exactly, hibernation. These animals wake up more easily during the winter and their body temperatures do not get as low as that of true hibernators.

Those That Endure   Still other animals don't avoid winter by migrating or by hibernating. They remain active or semi-active all winter long. White-tailed deer dine on tender tree branches and paw holes in the snow to get to grass underneath. Squirrels, when not snoozing, feast off stored nuts or whatever they can find. Birds eat what berries are left on the trees. Foxes, bobcats, and other predators depend on thick winter fur to keep them warm as they hunt rabbits, squirrels, and other prey in the snow.

GETTING A DRINK AND A MEAL

Water is a basic animal need. Many creatures get some water from the moist berries and insects they eat. Others, such as raccoons or deer, also seek pond or stream water to slake their thirst. For a squirrel, a mouse, or a small bird, a drink of water from a puddle, or a sip of dew off a leaf may serve as a thirst quencher. Then all they need is food. In the temperate deciduous forest, the many adaptations animals have evolved to get food is nothing short of amazing.

A Berry Good Meal   Temperate deciduous forests don't have many large, lush fruits like tropical forests do. But these forests do have berries—lots of them. Dogwood, spicebush, raspberry, cherry, tupelo, American bittersweet, strawberry, and countless other plants bear blue, orange, purple, red, or white berries. Flocks of cedar waxwings descend on such bushes with regularity. Squirrels, chipmunks, raccoons, bears, and even humans gobble up berries by the handful, jawful, and pawful when they're in season. But why do the plants "bother" to produce berries? Berries contain the seeds of the plant. The tiny seeds pass through the animals' digestive systems and are deposited in feces. There, with the feces providing a handy packet of fertilizer, the seeds can sprout and grow. In this way, plants let animals do the work of spreading their seeds.

Nuts About Nuts   Chestnuts, beechnuts, acorns, and chinquapins are just a sampling of the nutritious nuts found in a temperate deciduous forest. Squirrels, turkeys, raccoons, deer, and mice all dine on nuts. Unlike berries, the seed portion of a nut is destroyed when an animal eats it. But fortunately, animals aren't tidy diners. They scatter, bury, and forget many nuts along the way. These nuts sprout and grow. Oak trees produce large numbers of acorns every few years. This superabundance of acorns overwhelms the

Berries of the American bittersweet vine are an important part of this cedar waxwing's diet.

squirrels and other creatures, which can't eat all of the nuts at once. In those years, many more nuts may survive to sprout.

Leafy Lunches   Insect larvae such as caterpillars are the primary leaf eaters in the temperate deciduous forest. Except for an occasional nibbling deer or woodchuck, leaves aren't eaten much by mammals. Bark, however, makes a good feast for porcupines, deer, and other creatures. And young, tender twigs are fair game for hungry beavers or deer.

Natural Sweets   Abundant blooming trees and wildflowers provide nectar and pollen to forest residents. Bees gather pollen to feed to their larvae, and chew up nectar to form it into honey. Hummingbirds, butterflies, and moths dine on the flower nectar feast.

Insects à la Carte   Whether it's beetles under bark, caterpillars served up on a green leaf, or butterflies caught in

35

midair, insects are just about the most popular meat "dish" in the temperate deciduous forest. Birds fly thousands of miles from South America just to feast on the insect abundance in the temperate deciduous forest. And the many ways birds have adapted to catch their meals is remarkable. Towhees scratch back and forth in the dirt to get beetles, ants, and grubs. Worm-eating warblers and kinglets flutter their wings along leaves to rustle up insects to eat. Flycatchers nab insects in midair. And brown creepers, sapsuckers, nuthatches, and various woodpeckers methodically search tree branches and trunks for insects.

Ant Lions and Web Weavers   Animals without beaks get in on the insect feast as well. The larvae of the ant lion builds a sloping sandpit and waits at the bottom. When an unwary insect comes along, and falls down the sloping pit, the ant lion has a meal. Web-weaving spiders trap insects with almost invisible webs hung from trees. They unwittingly provide for hummingbirds, which have been known to swoop down and snatch trapped insects from spiderwebs.

Jaws, Claws, and Talons   Plenty of other predators, from screech owls to gray foxes, inhabit the temperate deciduous forest. Many of these predators rely on strong muscles and sharp claws, teeth, and talons to catch a meal. Coyotes, foxes, weasels, hawks, and owls are among the common predators. Bobcats also stalk the forest, hunting mice, voles, rats, quail, squirrels, rabbits, and other prey. Large predators in these forests typically can eat many different kinds of prey, hunting whatever is most abundant in a certain season or year.

Rotten Tastes   Scavengers are creatures that have a taste for something rotten. Turkey vultures eat dead animals— animals killed by predators or animals that died from sickness or injury. To do this cleanup job, the vulture has a strong stomach; it can eat food so rotten it would kill a human being. To defend itself, a vulture vomits on its attacker. (Considering how smelly and vile the food was even before the vulture ate it, you can see why vulture vomit might make an attacker run for cover!) Just about the only animals that will eat what a vulture leaves behind are insects, earthworms, and bacteria. These decomposers break down dead plants and animals into soil. Fungi also help in the decomposition job; but they are neither plants nor animals. They belong to a kingdom all their own.

ANIMAL SHELTERS, ANIMAL HOMES

In addition to water and food, many animals also seek shelter—a place where they can hole up for the winter, stay dry on a rainy day, or raise young in a warm, hidden, protected place.

Rollers, Builders, and Spitters   Lots of insects don't need anything fancy for shelter. A rolled-up leaf, the underside of a piece of bark, or the inside of a stem may be a fine place to spend the winter, lay eggs, or change into an adult. Some insects build more complex shelters, such as the corrugated adobe columns of the mud wasps' home. Spittlebug nymphs have an unusual habit. They cover themselves with white, frothy spitlike bubbles that help to hide them and keep them moist while they suck plant juices from stems.

What a Lot of Gall!   Have you ever seen strange swellings on the leaves, stems, or branches of a plant? They were probably galls. Certain species of fly, bee, beetle, wasp, butterfly, and moth stimulate plants to make galls. Galls form when an insect bores into a plant, irritating the plant's tissues. This causes the plant to grow a large tumorous growth—a gall. Galls are useful to insects in many different ways. The inside of a gall can be a convenient, protected

Some moth species transform from
caterpillars to winged adults inside galls.

place for an insect to lay its eggs. Galls are also used as a place for metamorphosis—where an insect can turn from a moth caterpillar, for instance, into an adult, winged moth.

Lots of Cavities   Many birds don't build nests on branches; they create cavities within trees. Woodpeckers and some nuthatches and chickadees excavate tree limb homes, flake by flake. Swallows, titmice, and wrens use cavities abandoned by cavity excavators, or naturally occurring holes in trees. Barn owls and raccoons look for ready-made cavities in the rotted out centers of dead trees. And other animals find shelter in underground burrows, cliff-top nests, leaf piles, twig piles, and countless different places.

TRICKERY AND FOOLERY IN THE FOREST

As if finding food, water, and shelter weren't enough of a problem, animals have to avoid predators along the way, too. Many have evolved camouflage—colors, shapes, and textures that help them stay hidden. But camouflage isn't useful just for prey animals hiding from predators. Camouflage is also a great way for predators to stay hidden as they sneak up on unsuspecting prey.

One common kind of camouflage is mimicry. Mimicry means an animal has evolved to look like—to mimic—a plant or another animal. Here are a few of the mimics you'll find in temperate deciduous forests and adjoining fields.

Leaf, Bark, and Twig Mimics   Looking like a plant is a great way to hide from enemies. Flattened, veined, and colored bright green, leaf look-alikes such as katydids and praying mantises can be hard to find among leaves. Smaller, darker, with a sharply humped back, insects called thorn-mimic treehoppers are hard to distinguish from thorns. And walking sticks, insects that resemble slender twigs, look right at home on a tree.

Flower Mimics   If you're an insect eater and you hide in a flower, your meals will come to you! The yellow coloring of the goldenrod spider and the yellow ambush bug allow these predators to hide and wait in goldenrod flowers. Hidden by their camouflage, they can pounce upon insects that visit the flower for nectar or pollen.

Butterfly Mimics   Why mimic a butterfly? So you can look like you taste bad. Monarch butterflies taste bad to birds. Once a bird eats one, it's not likely to eat another. It's also not likely to eat any viceroy butterflies, because viceroys have evolved to look like monarchs.

Bee and Wasp Mimics   To be a bee, or not to be . . . Many of the insects you think are bees and wasps probably aren't. Look closely. Drone flies, bee flies, tachinid flies, and hover flies all look like bees or wasps. Some take advantage of the

· THE SNEAKY COWBIRD AND THE DISAPPEARING MIGRANTS ·

Where have the birds gone? Ask a cowbird. In the last few years, birdwatchers have noticed fewer migrating songbirds arriving in the forests of the United States and Canada each spring. At least 30 percent of the bird species that migrate from Central and South America to the United States have significantly declined in number.

According to scientists, one reason for the birds' decline is the destruction of the tropical forests where these birds spend most of the year. But just as important, if not more important, is the destruction of their breeding grounds: the temperate deciduous forest in the United States. Over the years much of this forest has been cut down or sliced into smaller tracts by roads, developments, and logging.

Part of the problem is that there isn't enough space to nest. But an equally serious problem is that animals that prey on or parasitize songbirds have increased in population. These animals, such as raccoons, crows, blue jays, house cats, dogs, and cowbirds, are more common in "edge" habitats, where forests mix with fields and human habitation. These habitats are created when areas are developed, forest patches clear-cut, roads built, and so on.

Most of these problem animals, such as raccoons, crows, blue jays, dogs, and cats, eat birds and birds' eggs. But cowbirds threaten bird population in another way. They are nest parasites. Female cowbirds sneak their young into other birds' nests, sometimes removing one of the other birds' eggs to make room for their own. To make matters worse, the cowbird egg usually hatches first, so the young cowbird grows bigger and stronger than its nestmates.

Eventually, the nesting mother bird—even a tiny warbler—ends up struggling to feed the big, hungry cowbird while the other young die. Already, the cowbirds' "sneaky" habit has contributed to the decline of the endangered Kirtland's warbler. Many other birds are decreasing in number because their nesting is unsuccessful.

bees' and wasps' stinging reputation, whether they themselves have stingers or not.

INTERDEPENDENCE

The animals of the temperate deciduous forest are adapted not only to the weather, climate, soil, and plants of the forest, but also to one another. Predators are adapted to hunt many different kinds of prey, because animals may be abundant in different seasons. Prey animals are adapted to escape from predators by running, flying, climbing, swimming, burrowing, hiding, or, in the case of skunks, stinking! Yet the connections among forest animals may be much more subtle. Skunks, raccoons, and foxes may live in a woodchuck's discarded den. A mouse may get its calcium from nibbling a deer's shed antlers, while a flycatcher uses the lightweight, strong fibers of spiderwebs to build its tiny nest. It is these kinds of connections that make the forest a complex, interwoven, living community.

6
TEMPERATE DECIDUOUS FOREST COMMUNITIES

It's likely that many of the oak trees you see in the forest grew from acorns planted by squirrels and chipmunks. Well, perhaps "planted" is not the right word. Forgotten may be a better description of how this happens. Squirrels and chipmunks bury nuts in the ground to store them. But they forget, and often can't find, many of the nuts they bury! Even their trusty sense of smell doesn't always lead them back to their cache. As a result, oak trees sprout and grow as if planted on purpose.

The temperate deciduous forest, and all biomes for that matter, are made up of such interconnections between plants and animals. Each animal, plant, fungus, and bacterium plays a role within a biological community. These connections are what make up the interwoven web of life in the temperate deciduous forest.

LAYERS OF LIFE

The temperate deciduous forest has layers. Tall maples, oaks, hickories, tulip poplars, and dozens of other trees create a canopy layer—a roof for the forest. Shorter trees such as dogwoods, redbuds, and American holly create a second layer of treetops—called the understory—just below. Closer to the ground, shrubs with such exotic names as witch hazel, spicebush, and Hercules'-club grow in a shrub layer. And even lower down, closer to the leaf-covered forest floor, mushrooms mingle with colorful wildflowers such as trout lily, lady's slipper, and larkspur. These ground-hugging plants make up the herb layer.

Like high-rise apartment buildings, the forest's layers allow many animals to live on a relatively small piece of land. Some animals stick to particular forest layers, while others range far and wide. Birds are active at all layers, although certain species feed at particular levels in the forest. Orioles and tanagers feed up in the canopy, nuthatches and woodcreepers wander up and down tree trunks, while towhees scratch for food on the ground. Squirrels range far and wide among the forest layers, usually nesting in the canopy, while certain mice species climb up into the shrub layer to obtain berries and other foods.

GO WITH THE FLOW

Energy flow is what links the animals and plants in a natural community. In the temperate deciduous forest, energy in the form of sunlight is used by a dogwood tree's leaves to make sugars, which are stored as starch in its leaves, roots, shoots, and seeds. When the dogwood berries are eaten by a cardinal, some of the energy in the berries becomes part of the cardinal. (Some of that energy is also dissipated as heat, as it is every time energy is transferred from one organism to another.) So when a hawk eats that cardinal, some of that energy becomes part of the hawk. Finally, when the hawk dies, scavengers such as turkey vultures eat its body, and some of that energy becomes part of them. Decomposers—worms, bacteria, fungi, and small insects—finish up the job, using the rest. The leftovers and by-products of their meals become part of the soil.

Lots of Rot Dead animals and leaves can usually rot within a few weeks or months in the temperate deciduous forest during the warmth of summer. This decomposition generally takes longer than in the tropical rain forest, but less time than it takes in the taiga or tundra. How quickly leaves decompose depends on the air temperature, moisture, how thickly the leaves are packed, the decomposers at work, and the chemical contents of the leaves. Because they contain a chemical called tannin, oak leaves may remain well preserved on the forest floor for a year or more.

Energetic Ideas   A simple diagram of energy links, such as the ones described above, is called a food chain. Several food chains, linked together, create a food web—a diagram ecologists use to show the energy relationships among many organisms in a community. All the energy in a food web comes originally from sunlight. Because of its position on the earth, the temperate deciduous forest receives plenty of natural energy in the form of sunlight. This is different from the tundra and taiga, which receive much less sunlight energy in a year.

• FISH, FISHERMEN, AND FALL •

What does good fishing have to do with fall leaves? Lots. Up to 99 percent of a stream's energy can come from the leaves, branches, and other forest tidbits that fall into it. In fall, leaves drop into the stream and decay. Bacteria and fungi feed on the leaves. Then insects nicknamed "shredders" shred the leaves, eating both leaves and the fungi on the leaves. The shredders—stone fly nymphs, isopods, crane fly larvae, and others—are favorite foods for fish. And when their numbers decrease, so do fish populations.

That's just one of the many reasons removing streamside trees and other plants can cause real trouble for the entire stream community, including fish. So if you want good fishing, or simply a healthy stream, protect the forest on its banks as well.

MEASURES OF LIFE

It's obvious when you look at a temperate deciduous forest that there's more "stuff" growing in it than grows in a desert. To measure such a difference, biologists measure plant biomass—the weight of the roots, shoots, leaves, tree trunks, and other plant material that exist in a certain area. Temperate deciduous forests are heavy with plant matter, having as much as 385,000 pounds per acre (431,000 kilograms per hectare) of plant biomass in very old forests. About 30 percent of the forest's plant biomass is belowground, in the form of roots, or underground stems.

DIVERSITY

It's not uncommon to find several dozen tree species on a walk through a forest in southern Appalachia. That's because temperate deciduous forests have a moderate plant diversity—a fairly large number of plant species. This diversity is in great contrast to the taiga, where there may be only three or four tree species for hundreds of miles. Only tropical rain forests harbor more tree species than temperate deciduous forests.

Yet when it comes to mammal species, the temperate deciduous forest is a mixed bag. With only bear, deer, and in northern parts, moose, the temperate deciduous forest has fewer large mammal species than the taiga. On the other hand, the temperate deciduous forest has more species of smaller mammals such as squirrels and mice. However, arboreal mammals—mammals that spend most of their time up in trees—are unusually scarce, when you consider how many monkeys, sloths, and other arboreal mammals live in tropical rain forests.

Reptile and amphibian species, particularly salamanders, are especially diverse in the temperate deciduous forest. The Blue Ridge Mountains in Virginia are home to what amounts to the salamander capital of the world—a place where many species of hard-to-find amphibians live near streams and on other parts of the wet forest floor. Bird species, too, are diverse in the temperate deciduous forests. But many of these birds are migrants—spending only summers there, and the rest of their time in the tropics. When it comes to species diversity, temperate deciduous forests are "in-between." Overall, they have a species diversity higher than taiga, but lower than tropical rain forests.

TAKE A HIKE IN THE TEMPERATE DECIDUOUS FOREST

As in any other biome, you should dress for the weather in the temperate deciduous forest. Bring warm clothes, a light jacket in summer, and many warm layers in winter. Know where you're going, tell someone of your plans, bring a map, and carry enough food and water to keep your energy level high. Lightweight long pants and a long-sleeved shirt should help prevent bug bites and poison ivy. But it's best to know what poison ivy looks like and avoid it when possible. And it's good to check for ticks when you return from your hike.

Here are just a few of the things you can look for, smell for, and listen for on a temperate deciduous forest hike:

- The deep twangs of frogs calling for mates;
- Bright dogwood berries on trees;
- The shed skin of a snake;
- Deep marks on trees, where a black bear has sharpened its claws;
- Spiral trails of beetles' gnawings under bark;
- Footprints of a raccoon near a stream's edge;
- Owl pellets—oblong, compressed bits of fur and bones;
- Leafy nests of squirrels high in the trees;
- Rows of holes on tree trunks, where woodpeckers have searched for bugs;
- Fragrant leaves of spicebush or peppermint.

FOREST TYPES

Scientists divide temperate deciduous forests into several different types, according to what trees dominate the forest. These forest types are called associations. In the north, beech/maple forests are common. The oak/hickory association extends westward from Appalachia to the Great Lakes. Before the decline of the chestnut tree, an oak/chestnut association was common from the southeast, north to New York and New Jersey.

In Appalachia and in the Cumberland Plateau area of West Virginia, you'll find the mixed mesophytic association. This type of forest is called mesophytic because it requires a medium amount of moisture. It is called mixed because it is dominated not by one or two tree species, but by any one of ten or so species. Although all these types are named only for their trees, many other plants and animals dwell in association with these dominant trees, hence the name "association."

SUCCESSION

More than 80 percent of the temperate deciduous forest in the United States has been cut for timber, cleared for agriculture, or burned by fire in the last few hundred years. What we think of as temperate deciduous forest is mostly secondary growth—what has regrown on the original land. Fortunately, unlike many tropical rain forest soils, temperate deciduous forest soils are fertile enough, in general, to allow forest regrowth.

But a thick, oak/hickory forest or maple/beech forest doesn't immediately sprout and grow on cleared land. The land goes through stages as it returns to forest, in a process called succession. First, sun-loving, quick-sprouting meadow plants such as goldenrod and ragweed fill in the cleared area. Then, longer-lasting grasses and other small plants grow. These plants change the soil in such a way that sapling trees such as pine and birch can become established.

Under the shelter of these trees, shade-loving trees such as oaks thrive. They can grow up tall and eventually shade out the trees that once sheltered them. And so the oak / hickory forest returns. A similar successional sequence can return maple / beech forest, too.

The steps above are a generalized version of succession. How it works, in practice, depends on factors such as how damaged the forest is in the beginning, how fertile the soil is, and the proximity of seed sources—other forest patches.

A TRICK OF ALTITUDE

Even in the middle of the temperate deciduous forest, you may be able to get a peek at other biomes such as the taiga and tundra. By climbing a high mountain, you can reach altitudes where climatic conditions mimic those of places hundreds, or even thousands, of miles north. At the top of such a mountain may be a snowy, barren zone, which is much like the high Arctic, or polar desert. Farther down you'll find fields of low-growing plants. This community is called the alpine tundra, which is much like Arctic tundra. Below this altitude, at the timberline, conifer forests much like the taiga clothe the mountainside. And when you climb back down the mountain, you can reach the broad-leafed trees of the temperate deciduous forest once again.

PEOPLE AND THE TEMPERATE DECIDUOUS FOREST

When English settlers arrived on North America's shores 300 years ago, they saw a forest far different from the one we see today. Moose lived on Long Island, cougars roamed Connecticut, and bison wandered forests from Pennsylvania to Georgia. Trees towered to heights of 100 or more feet (30 or more meters). Elk, turkeys, beavers, otters, bears, cougars, and wolves were abundant. And passenger pigeons were so numerous, their mile-wide flocks darkened the sky and stretched for hundreds of miles. The temperate deciduous forest was indeed a vast, wondrous place, rich with wildlife.

ANCIENT FOREST PEOPLE

Despite its richness, the forest those first European settlers saw was not untouched by humans. On the contrary, Native Americans had been living in North America's forests for thousands of years. But their numbers were small, and their way of life had little negative impact, overall, on the forest.

Native Americans survived by hunting deer, squirrels, and bear from the forests. They gathered leaves, nuts, roots, and berries, and they grew corn, squash, beans, and tobacco. Although Native Americans did cut, clear, burn, and farm within the forest, in most cases they only did so on small plots of land. And after eight to ten years, they abandoned most plots, letting the forest fill in and regrow.

THE FALL OF THE FOREST AND ITS PEOPLE

In the 100 years from 1870 to 1970, most of the temperate deciduous forest was cut down. Approximately 500 million acres (200 million hectares) of the eastern forest in the United States were clear-cut. All of the trees were cut down. Open land and lumber were needed to build houses, factories, and other facilities as the United States grew. Forest was cleared for agriculture.

The government encouraged Europeans to settle land, giving them ownership only of land they "improved." Unfortunately, improving the land usually meant cutting down trees to clear land for homes or agriculture. Only in remote, mountainous areas, where hillsides were steep enough to make farming and logging impractical, did forests remain untouched.

For American wildlife, this deforestation was a disaster. Millions of animals lost their habitat. Wood bison and elk died out. State governments paid bounties for the shooting of thousands of wolves and cougars. And because of habitat loss and hunting, the passenger pigeon—once among the most abundant birds on the continent—became extinct by 1913.

As the temperate deciduous forest was destroyed, the Native Americans who lived there suffered, too. In various wars and conflicts, many were killed outright by Europeans. Others died because of diseases brought into the country by the new settlers. And many Native Americans were moved by the government to reservations on less desirable lands farther west. The other changes Europeans brought to America—the new towns, the new industries, the liquor, and the gambling—all took their toll on Native American families and their way of life.

SIGNS OF RECOVERY AND REGROWTH

Today, Native Americans who originated in the temperate deciduous forest live in all walks of life, and work in many different careers, all over the country. Some live an almost entirely modern life, but take time to gather at powwows, where they dress in traditional clothing, dance, sing, tell stories, and celebrate the culture they share. A number of Native Americans live on reservations such as the Cherokee reservation near Gatlinburg, Tennessee. And some retain close ties to their culture, carrying out religious rites and practicing traditional arts such as pottery, basketry, bead-work, hunting, and native medicine. In recent years, Native American groups in many biomes, all around the United States, have been joining forces to reassert their rights to their land and their cultural identity.

Native Plants   In some parts of the United States, the temperate deciduous forests are recovering. In general, forests regrow faster on lands that have been logged or burned rather than those that have been cleared, plowed, and used for farming. However, forests can eventually reestablish themselves even on old farm fields, as long as the soil is in good health. Indeed, in New England, there is more forest today than there was 100 years ago! That's because 100 years ago much New England forest had already been cleared for small farms. But when larger, mechanized farms in the Midwest began providing inexpensive food for the country, small farms in New England declined. Forests regrew on old farm fields.

Native Animals   With a little help, several wildlife species are bouncing back. Wild turkeys, which used to wander deciduous forests in flocks of hundreds but then declined, are slowly increasing in number because of reintroduction programs that breed wild turkeys in captivity then release them into the wild. In Shenandoah National Park, bear populations had drastically decreased, but now that they are protected from hunting, they are recovering. And river otters, which had died out because of overhunting and polluted streams, have been successfully reintroduced to the Great Smoky Mountains, where they were once extinguished by hunters.

CONSERVATION THREATS TO THE FOREST

Despite the signs of forest recovery, there remain many serious threats to the health and future survival of the remaining forest.

Acid Rain and Other Air Pollution   On mountaintops in the southern Appalachians, whole groves of trees are dead and dying, leaving leafless, skeletonlike trees. The underlying cause of tree death seems to be pollution, specifically acid rain and ozone. Sulfates and other chemicals from running cars, power plants, and factories combine with rain to form these harmful pollutants.

Mountaintop trees are particularly likely to suffer damage because they are frequently bathed in harmful, acidic fogs, and experience high ozone levels. On the western side of Mount Mitchell in North Carolina, one-half of the red spruce and fir are dead. In the northeastern United States, broad-leafed trees such as birch, beech, ash, and maple are also showing signs of decline. It is difficult to prove that air pollution kills the trees outright. But scientists have found that air pollution weakens the health of trees, which makes them more likely to die from insects, cold, disease, and other natural causes.

Oh, Deer!   Hard as it may be to believe, deer are a major threat to the native plants and animals of the temperate deciduous forest. Without natural predators, which were killed off long ago, deer populations have skyrocketed in the past few decades. Deer overpopulation is a problem, especially in parks where hunting is not allowed.

Deer can reduce a healthy forest, full of wildflowers, to a collection of trees with an almost bare forest floor. Trillium

Lady's slippers are among the rare wildflowers that are wiped out in areas where deer are too plentiful.

and spring beauties are among the first wildflowers to get wiped out, because they are favorite deer foods. How bad is the problem? Well, to find out, a scientist fenced off a forest area to keep out deer. His results: the deer-free area inside the fence had three times more low-growing plant matter than the deer-grazing area outside. In a healthy forest, these low-growing plants provide food and shelter for small animals such as turtles and birds.

Logging Clear-cutting of forest continues on private lands and in national forests in the eastern deciduous forest. This lumber is used to build houses and make products people use every day. But many environmentalists believe the amount of lumber harvested from the national forests is too high. The trees replanted on forest land are of only a few species. So what regrows is more like a farm field of certain trees than a forest, full of many different animal and plant species.

Global Climate Change   High above the earth is a layer of naturally occurring gases. These greenhouse gases act like the glass panes of a greenhouse, allowing sunlight into the earth's atmosphere, but allowing only some of the sunlight-generated heat to escape. These gases keep the earth warm. But the problem today is that the quantity of these gases in the atmosphere has increased dramatically. Much of this extra gas comes from people's activities—cattle ranching, industrial plants, automobiles, and the burning of tropical forests. Scientists aren't sure exactly how all these greenhouse gases will change the earth's climate and affect the animals and plants of the temperate deciduous forest. But they are concerned because the increased carbon dioxide does affect plant growth.

Development   Ski slopes, mountain retreats, homes, shopping malls, amusement parks—such development involves cutting down forest and clearing land. These days many people are rushing to the mountains, forests, and countryside to escape crowded city life. But as a result, they are building on and destroying some forest land.

Water Pollution   Streams are an important part of the temperate deciduous forest biome. Unfortunately, they're being polluted. During timber cutting and development, trees and other plants are often cut away from streambanks. This deprives stream insects of leafy nourishment. It also leads to pollution when soil washes off bare banks, choking stream life. Other sources of pollution include industrial outflow and runoff of pesticides and fertilizers from farms, lawns, and other developments.

Illegal Harvest of Plants and Animals   Despite the Endangered Species Act of 1973 and other laws protecting forest wildlife, illegal trade in rare plant and animal species

· SAVE YOUR STREAMS ·

How can you test a stream for pollution? One way is to test the water chemically in a laboratory. Problem is, there are thousands of possible pollutants. Testing for all of them is time-consuming and expensive. So, people who want to monitor the health of a stream often take another approach. They find out what lives in the stream. Certain animals thrive in, or can at least tolerate, polluted water. Others die in even slightly polluted water.

Pollution-sensitive organisms such as the stone fly, caddis fly, riffle beetle, mayfly, and gilled snail are found only in very good quality water. Less-sensitive organisms such as crayfish, sow bugs, damselflies, beetle larvae, and clams can tolerate water of fair quality. And aquatic worms, blackfly larva, leeches, and pond snails can tolerate quite a lot of pollution, and so can be found in good, fair, or poor quality water.

To learn how to net and identify these stream inhabitants, contact the Izaak Walton League about a Save Our Streams workshop. They train civic or school groups to be "stream watchers": to periodically examine a stream's water and the organisms in it. Pollution data gathered is then given to county and state environmental officials to warn them of possible pollution problems. For information on how your group can join the Save Our Streams program, contact:

Izaak Walton League of America, SOS Program
1401 Wilson Boulevard, Level B
Arlington, VA 22209-2318
Phone 1-703-528-1818

continues. Black bear paws, gallbladders, and other body parts are sold to Asian clients to be made into folk medicines popular in China and Japan. Rare wildflowers are dug up from parks and national forests and sold for landscaping.

Introduced Species   For the temperate deciduous forest of the southern Appalachians, wild boars are a disaster on the hoof. Sometime around 1912, these nonnative animals escaped from a game reserve in North Carolina. Today, herds of these wild boars roam the forest, rooting and digging up whatever they can find to eat—from roots to berries to nuts. Voracious eaters, the wild boars tear up and trample fragile wildflowers, damage shrubs and trees, and muddy streams. They also compete with bears and squirrels, eating the same foods. So far park rangers have been unsuccessful in stopping the ever-expanding wild boar population. How serious is the problem? Some years the Great Smoky Mountains National Park spends $200,000 just trying to remove these hogs.

Mining   Mining for coal, granite, and other resources involves stripping off forest to get to the rock underneath. Many acres of mining lands become damaged to the extent that forests do not regrow on the depleted soils.

Off-road Vehicles   Off-road vehicles such as motorbikes are a threat to forest areas, especially when ridden off designated trails. These machines tear up fragile plants, crush animal burrows, scare wildlife, and increase erosion. They also ruin the quiet solitude many people seek in forest lands.

HOPE FOR THE FUTURE

The list of problems facing the forest is lengthy. But don't be overwhelmed. A healthy future for temperate deciduous forests *is* possible. People all over the United States are working on solutions. Here are just a few of the actions people are taking to safeguard temperate deciduous forests:

- Members of a program called Global ReLeaf are planting native trees to reforest land.
- Forest Watch citizen volunteers are working side by side with Forest Service employees, giving them input on how they would like the forests managed. Volunteers regularly hike through forests to pinpoint special problems, and advise the Forest Service concerning timber sales.
- An organization called the Association of Forest Service Employees for Environmental Ethics is helping forest managers do their jobs. This organization makes sure that foresters who support environmental efforts will not lose their jobs for speaking out.
- As part of a national program called Kidsnet, students around the country are learning how to test the acidity of local rainwater, stream water, and lake water. They're sharing their information with environmental officials and with one another, through National Geographic Kidsnet, a computer network.
- The Nature Conservancy is buying and preserving small forest plots with special ecological value. These areas are often home to rare plants and animals.

With these and other creative approaches to conservation problems, scientists feel there's a chance that much of the remaining temperate deciduous forest can be preserved. But a healthy future for these forests will require expanding conservation efforts. More people will need to get involved. For information on how *you* can help, read the next section!

RESOURCES AND WHAT
YOU CAN DO TO HELP

Here's what you can do to help ensure that temperate deciduous forests are conserved:

• Learn more by reading books and watching videos and television programs about the temperate deciduous forest. Check your local library, bookstore, and video store for resources. Here are just a few of the books available for further reading:

Eastern Forests by Ann Sutton and Myron Sutton (The
    Audubon Society Nature Guides Series) (Knopf, 1985).
Field Guide to Eastern Forests by John C. Cricher (Peterson
    Field Guide Series) (Houghton Mifflin, 1988).
The Field Guide to Wildlife Habitats of the Eastern United States
    by Janine M. Benyus (Simon & Schuster, 1989).
Forests: A Naturalist's Guide to Trees & Forest Ecology by
    Laurence C. Walker (John Wiley and Sons, Inc., 1990).
Once upon a Tree: Life from Treetop to Root Tips by James B.
    Nardi (Iowa State University Press, 1993).

• For more information on temperate deciduous forest and temperate deciduous forest related issues, write or call the following organizations:

Forest Watch
The Wilderness Society
900 17th Street, NW
Washington, DC 20006-2596
Phone 1-202-833-2300

Global ReLeaf
American Forests
1516 P Street, NW
Washington, DC 20005
Phone 1-202-667-3300

If you like the job these organizations are doing, consider becoming a member.

• Visit a museum, national park, national monument, or botanical garden that has temperate deciduous forest features or displays. The following United States national parks, national forests, and state parks contain temperate deciduous forest:

Adirondack Forest Preserve, Ray Brook, NY
Chequamegon National Forest, Park Falls, WI
Cherokee National Forest, Cleveland, TN
Great Smoky Mountains National Park, Gatlinburg, TN
Hot Springs National Park, Hot Springs, AR
Monongahela National Forest, Elkins, WV
Ozark-St. Francis National Forest, Russellville, AR
Pisgah National Forest, Asheville, NC
Shenandoah National Park, Luray, VA

• Educate others about the temperate deciduous forest. Put on a skit at school, or construct a display for the hallway or a local mall to raise awareness of forest issues.

• Your class may want to join the National Geographic Society's Kidsnet, a computer-based acid rain testing network. For information, contact:

The National Geographic Society
Attention: Educational Services
P.O. Box 98018
Washington, DC 20090
Phone 1-800-368-2728

• Write letters to state and national government officials, telling them you feel temperate deciduous forest conservation is important.

• Turn off lights, televisions, and other appliances when you are not using them. Saving electricity can prevent the need for coal mining, which damages temperate deciduous forest. Encourage your family to use energy-saving devices in your home. For more energy-saving tips, contact your local electric utility. For a catalog of energy-saving appliances and other environmental products, write or call:

Real Goods
966 Mazzoni Street
Ukiah, CA 95482-3471
Phone 1-800-762-7325

Seventh Generation
Colchester, VT 05446-1672
Phone 1-800-456-1177

• Recycle paper and other products. Recycling uses less energy and fewer trees than making a product from scratch. Also, buy recycled products.

GLOSSARY

abscission layer a layer of cells across the base of a leaf stem; when this layer dehydrates, and wind blows, the leaf falls from the tree

acid rain a general term for precipitation that has been acidified by pollution in the air

association a plant community characterized by its dominant tree types

biome an area that has a certain kind of climate and a certain kind of community of plants and animals

clear-cutting cutting all the trees from an area of land

deciduous plants that drop all their leaves each year

ecotone a border between two biomes, where the plants and animals of those biomes mingle

ephemerals plants that sprout, grow, flower, set seed, and die back quickly

evergreen plants that keep their leaves for more than one year

fragmentation the division of a large portion (in this case, forest) into smaller pieces

hardening a process by which a plant changes its internal chemistry in order to avoid frost damage during winter

hibernate to enter a winter state of inactivity that involves a substantial drop in body temperature

humidity   the amount of water vapor in the air at a certain temperature, as compared to how much water vapor the air can hold at that temperature

humus   a layer of well-decomposed plant and animal matter

mesophytic   having a moderate amount of water in the environment

mimicry   imitation of an object's or another organism's shape, form, color, or behavior

phloem   a system of cells that carry food throughout a plant

plant biomass   the weight of all the plant matter—roots, shoots, stems, and other plant parts—for a given area

secondary forests   forests that have regrown on logged or cleared land

species diversity   the number of different kinds of plants and animals in a given place

succession   the process by which a sequence of plant communities naturally replace one another in a given area

taiga   a biome that is characterized by evergreen conifers such as spruce and fir, and occurs north of the temperate deciduous forest

temperate deciduous forest   a biome supporting broad-leafed trees that drop their leaves in fall

torpor   a sluggish condition that is not sleep or a hibernating state

tropical rain forest   natural evergreen forest located in the tropics and characterized by high rainfall

xylem   a system of cells that carry water throughout a plant

INDEX